I0102663

Politics and Culture in African Emancipatory Politics

Two Perspectives:

Amílcar Cabral
(1972)
Ernest Wamba-dia-Wamba
(2003)

Edited by
Michael Neocosmos

Daraja Press

Published by
Daraja Press
https://darajapress.com

ISBN: 9781990263330

Introduction: © 2021 Michael Neocosmos
The role of culture in the struggle for independence by Amílcar Cabral
   originally published in French by UNESCO (https://unesdoc.un-
   esco.org/ark:/48223/pf0000001749). The text here was translated
   by Michael Neocosmos.
The Mbongi and the Palaver yesterday, today and tomorrow by Ernest
   Wamba-dia-Wamba (previously in French, unpublished). This
   translation by Michael Neocosmos. © 2021 Estate of Ernest
   Wamba-dia-Wamba.

Cover illustrations: Anastasya Eliseeva
Cover design: Kate McDonnell

Library and Archives Canada Cataloguing in Publication
Title: Politics and Culture in
African Emancipatory Politics: two perspectives : Amílcar Cabral (1972), Ernest
   Wamba dia Wamba (2003).
Names: Container of (work): Cabral, Amílcar, 1924-1973. Cultura nacional. English. I
   Container of (work): Wamba-dia-Wamba, E. Mbongi and the palaver. I Neocos-
   mos, M., writer of introduction.
Description: Series statement: Thinking freedom
Identifiers: Canadiana 20210365064 I ISBN 9781990263330 (softcover)
Subjects: LCSH: Politics and culture—Africa. I LCSH: Popular culture—Africa. I
   LCSH: National   liberation movements—Africa.
Classification: LCC JA75.7 .A37 2021 I DDC 306.2096—dc23

Contents

Introduction..1
  Michael Neocosmos

The role of culture in the struggle for independence.........21
  Amílcar Cabral

The Mbongi and the Palaver yesterday, today and
tomorrow:..41
  Ernest Wamba dia Wamba

Introduction

Michael Neocosmos[1]

the masses are the bearers of culture, they are themselves its source, and at the same time, the only entity truly capable of preserving and creating this culture, of making history (A. Cabral)

The profound meaning of dictatorship in Africa is the imposition of this graft [state] on the whole of society, by means that aim at the violent and vicious destruction of peasant culture and traditions. [...] It is a deep civilizational crisis. The three African refusals can be explained on this basis: the refusal to think for oneself, the refusal to take seriously all of one's past and the refusal to see things in a long-term perspective. We speak with borrowed speeches, sometimes without being aware of it. (E. Wamba-dia-Wamba)

The immediate aim of this introduction is to outline two views of the importance of popular African cultures in the changing contexts of thinking political emancipation on the continent. It was decided to take one conception from the twentieth century and one from the twenty-first because of the different ways in which emancipatory politics has been thought in different historical periods, although it will be noticed how both are inspired by a dialectical mode of thought. The essay by Cabral is firmly focussed on thinking liberation from colonialism (the domination of a foreign colonial state) and the potential importance of African cultures in this process. Wamba-dia-Wamba piece considers the potential for emancipation from neocolonialism and its attendant neoliberal conceptions of politics and the state. In each case the central idea concerns the elucidation of a collective politics from an activation of the potentialities of different aspects of popular culture but thought in different ways. Given the absence of

[1] Michael Neocosmos is Emeritus Professor in the Humanities at Rhodes University, South Africa

a colonial state on the continent today and its replacement by a neo-colonial one which reproduces many of its features and alters some within a different historical context, it is no longer justifiable to simply replicate uncritically those political conceptions which have shown themselves to have been appropriate at the time but limiting today. To do so would be to encourage a counterproductive dogmatism. It is clear, for example, that the party form of organisation – which was central to the thought of anticolonial struggles – is in crisis on the continent today because it no longer represents distinct classes or even different visions of the common good, but that it is simply a vehicle for private accumulation if not for the vulgar plunder of national resources that are then rapidly whisked out of the country.

In either case, the two political arguments discussed here insist on the centrality of culture in the politics of emancipation in Africa without collapsing into 'Afrocentrism' or 'nativism'. They do this by outlining distinct dialectical arguments that combine the particularity of culture and history with the universality of the human. Each will be discussed here with a view to elucidating a thought of politics that conceives of African cultures as possessing universal emancipatory potentials within particular cultural settings. These potentialities then require simultaneous activation by a mass movement. As part of this process, it will be argued that the subject of political knowledge is potentially already a collectivity, and that, therefore, the process of acquiring political knowledge is a collective and not an individual one. Africans are therefore potentially one step ahead of many peoples in the Global North, for example, as forms of acquiring collective knowledge and resolving popular differences have not yet been socially forgotten. Whereas for Cabral, culture constitutes the medium through which a mass politics can be developed so that a nation can recover its history through political action, for Wamba-dia-Wamba the primary process of politics is constituting such a political collective through resolving contradictions among the people by means of existing cultural prescriptions.

Amílcar Cabral: Popular culture and the re-appropriation of history through politics

Emancipatory struggles in Africa have been concerned precisely with reasserting the human in social relations and with the full insertion of African Peoples into a universal history from which they were forcibly excluded by colonialism and racial capitalism. The masses of the people have been and continue to be (despite consistent attempts at acculturation) the ultimate bearers of culture. As a result, their struggles regularly insisted on founding or re-asserting a philosophical anthropology from the cultures within which Africans lived. Yet, in the eyes of the nationalist leaders of the 1950s and 60s, these cultures were frequently contradictory, exhibiting both ethnic particularisms as well as potentialities for thinking the universal. Arguably, the dialectic of the culturally specific and the universally human was at the core of the thought of those few who took such cultural liberation seriously. Those few leaders who attempted to think the cultural potentiality for emancipation in Africa tended to do so after achieving state power. Particularly illustrative here was Nyerere's idea of Ujamaa, but most others attempted to overcome rather unsuccessfully what they saw as the divisive influences of colonially produced 'tribalism'. Emphatically affirming a Western conception of modernity, post-independence leaders overwhelmingly reduced popular culture to an ethnic problem, not to a popular solution (Neocosmos, 2016b, pp.480-485).

Yet there were exceptions, and some understood the dialectic between the struggle for a universal humanity and the centrality of culture in popular struggles. Foremost among these was Amílcar Cabral:

> We talk a lot about Africa, but we in our Party must remember that before being Africans we are men, human beings, who belong to the whole world. We cannot therefore allow any interest of our people to be restricted or thwarted because of our condition as Africans. We must put the interests of our people higher, in the context of the interests of mankind in general, and then we can put them in the context of the interests of Africa in general. (Cabral, 1979: 80)

Cabral discussed in detail the importance of African popular cultures in national liberation struggles and theorised a particular way of conceiving a politics of liberation at least partially founded upon popular cultures. What is particularly original is his attempt to combine a Leninist understanding of vanguard party politics with a mass cultural base among rural African societies. In attempting this approach to emancipatory politics, Cabral was very much a twentieth century thinker of national liberation. The centrality of the Leninist political party, the adherence to armed struggle and the insistence on iron party discipline, were all typical of that historically specific conception of anti-colonial emancipation.

Cabral insists that colonial state domination required colonial power to develop a knowledge of the culture of the colonised because, irrespective of its material forms, foreign domination could only be maintained through the destruction of indigenous culture.

> The practice of imperialist rule – its affirmation or its negation – required (and still requires) a more or less accurate knowledge of the dominated object and the historical reality (economic, social, and cultural) within which it moves, this knowledge necessarily being expressed in terms of comparison with the dominating subject and its historical reality. Such knowledge is an imperative necessity for the practice of imperialist rule, which usually results from the violent confrontation of two identities distinct in their historical content and antagonistic in their functions.

While this knowledge was an 'imperative necessity' for colonial control for Cabral, it was also acquired as an individual anthropological process, and in relation to the Western universal ('the dominating subject'). On the other hand, and in opposition to the efforts of the colonisers, Cabral argues that the rural masses among the colonised need to acquire an accurate knowledge of their struggle against colonial oppression as part of a collective practice in tandem with the leaders of the party of liberation.

Popular culture was thus a main intellectual and political concern of Cabral's throughout the anti-colonial struggle and he investigated cultures in some detail referring to social scientific writings in his investigations. The text discussed here was written very much like an academic paper (including footnotes and references) and was read on his behalf at a UNESCO meeting in 1972. It expands his work on culture written earlier in 1970 as National Liberation and Culture and published in the anthology Return to the Source in 1973.

Cabral's politics combined, to various extents, universalistic conceptions of humanity with narrower statist conceptions of liberation. This was because Cabral largely operated within a traditional Marxist perspective and a historicist conception of progress seen as resulting from the development of the productive forces/powers, but concurrently stressing culture not simply as a reflection or expression of the material base and classes, but as 'relatively autonomous' in Althusser's sense. He saw culture as 'simultaneously the fruit of a people's history and a determinant of history [though] like history, or because of its history, culture has as its material base the level of the productive forces and the mode of production' (Cabral, 1973: 41-42).

> History allows us to know the nature and extent of the imbalances and conflicts (economic, political and social) which characterize the evolution of a society; culture allows us to know the dynamic syntheses which have been developed and established by social consciousness to resolve these conflicts at each stage of its evolution, in the search for survival and progress (Cabral, 1973: 42, translation altered).

Culture for Cabral is thus the medium through which a collective socio-political consciousness is expressed (much like Emile Durkheim's 'conscience collective') and simultaneously points to culture's function of resolving conflicts which later becomes a dominant theme in the work of Wamba-dia-Wamba. It follows that it constitutes the language for thinking mass politics, although not party politics given that the latter is a vanguard and is hence steeped in Leninist vocabulary. [2]'Our struggle is based on our culture, because culture is the fruit of history and it is a strength' (Cabral, 1979: 58). Culture is the determi-

---

[2] For a more detailed discussion of the contradictory character of Cabral's politics see Neocosmos (2016a)

5

nant of a people's history precisely because it is political, and history is an effect of the re-appropriation of national collective politics.

Yet for Cabral not all culture is political in the sense of expressing popular resistance to colonial domination. In National Liberation and Culture, he says that 'liberation struggles are preceded by an increase in expressions of culture, consolidated progressively into a successful or unsuccessful attempt to affirm the cultural personality of the dominated people, as a means of negating the oppressor culture' (Cabral, 1973:43). When he comes to writing The Role of Culture in the Struggle for Independence, he rather emphasises from the very beginning that demonstrations of a cultural character or an apparent 'cultural renaissance' are not to be understood 'as a method of group mobilization and even a weapon in the fight for independence'. The political role of culture is more complex. For a start it fulfils different needs for different classes of the population, the urban petty-bourgeoisie and the rural masses.

> In order to acquire a correct appreciation of the true role of culture in the development of the liberation movement, a distinction must therefore be made, at least in Africa, between the situation of the masses who preserve their culture, and that of the social groups which are more or less assimilated, uprooted, and culturally alienated. Even though they may bear certain cultural features belonging to the native community, indigenous elites, themselves created by the colonizing process, live materially and spiritually the culture of the colonialist foreigner with whom they seek gradually to identify themselves in social behaviour and even in their view of indigenous cultural values.

In fact Cabral outlines the character of a decolonial politics in the strict sense *avant la lettre*. His is not an academic decolonial critique of Western conceptions in the Global South. Rather his is a political practice, what he terms a 'Return to the Source' which does not refer to going back to tradition but to integrating the political thought of the National Liberation Party-type Organisation (nb) within the fighting masses (i.e. within a mass movement). Although Cabral stressed on numerous occasions the importance of a vanguard party as opposed to a mass movement, one gets the distinct impression that he fears that the party form of organisation is, in part, a subjective bearer of statism. His formulation of 'the people recapturing their own history' should thus be read as the people becoming a collective political subject which was the only way they could become the subject of their own history and that of the progress of humanity as a whole. Yet, as we shall see, he is conscious of the fact that they may not succeed, especially after achieving independence. We of course know today that historicism is no longer tenable; humanity has not followed a road of historical progress. After all the people of Africa were systematically excluded from history also by the postcolonial state which purported to represent them. What Cabral, Fanon and others only envisaged as a possibility became a reality. The people's becoming a political subject was historically limited so that today, if we are to move beyond an understanding of history as progress, popular emancipatory politics must be understood as historically limited within sequences.[3]

One thus finds in Cabral's work an original inventive way of thinking mass politics whereby popular culture is understood as the element of national life necessary to resist the complete annihilation of Africanness and to provide a counterweight to the people's total assimilation into Western cultural norms led by the petty-bourgeoisie with the ultimate reproduction of colonial relations leading to neocolonialism. For Cabral it was not simply a matter of insisting on the specificity of an 'African personality' as in the work of Senghor and Nkrumah inter alia, nor was it a matter of counterposing an 'Afrocentrism' to a dominant 'Eurocentrism'.[4] Both of these were common positions at the time. Rather of central importance to Cabral was the immersion of the nationalist petty-bourgeoisie of the towns into the popular cultures of the rural areas in a process he referred to as a 'Return to the Source'. Closeness to the masses for Cabral was both a cultural and a political necessity. It was necessary in order to avert the assimilation and hence subservience of the African petty-bourgeoisie to the West, which he saw as the main danger confronting newly independent African states. It was also important because of the necessity to always keep in mind what one was fighting for: the liberation of the people themselves. For Cabral 'culture is simultaneously the fruit of a people's history and a

---

[3] See Michael Neocosmos (2016b).

[4] See Gordon (2008: 106-110); Sekyi-Otu (2018).

determinant of history' (p.41). If it is a determinant of history in the sense Cabral means it as a re-appropriation of national history which was blocked by colonialism, it is first and foremost a determinant of politics. Simply put it is only a political presence, i.e. the becoming of the nation as an independent political subject ('we the people') that enables the people to re-appropriate their history so that it is fully theirs to determine. Hence 'the people' is exclusively a political category:

> In Guiné and Cape Verde today the people... mean for us those who want to chase the Portuguese colonialists out of our land. They are the people, the rest are not of our land even if they were born there. They are not the people of our land; they are the population but not the people. This is what defines the people today (Cabral, 1979: 89).

Hence the question of who was a member of the people-nation required a purely political, not a social or historical answer.

> if imperialist domination has the vital need to practice cultural oppression, national liberation is necessarily an act of culture... The liberation movement must... embody the mass character, the popular character of the culture - which is not and never could be the privilege of one or of some sectors of the society (Cabral, 1973:43-4).

Yet the nation has a social foundation as the most consistently anti-colonial people are to be found among the masses, the poorest, the most excluded (the 'wretched of the earth') and particularly the rural peasantry. The nation has a bias towards the rural; not only are rural people a numerical majority, but they are the most politically excluded and oppressed. They have nothing to gain from the continuation of colonialism; only they can be truly universal and consistent in their demand for national freedom and democracy. But at the same time there is no guarantee that the people will be able to determine their own history after independence. Given that it is members of the petty-bourgeoisie who are likely to inherit the independent state, a 'return to the source' acquires even greater importance for the new state cannot be a simple question 'of a change of skin'.

> If you really want to know the feelings of our people on this matter I can tell you that our government and all its institutions have to take another nature. For example, we must not use the houses occupied by the colonial power in the way they used them. I proposed to our party that the government palace in Bissau be transformed into a people's house for culture, not for our prime minister or something like this (I don't believe we will have prime ministers anyway). This is to let the people realise that they conquered colonialism - it's finished this time - it's [not] only a question of a change of skin. This is really very important. It is the most important problem in the liberation movement. The problem of the nature of the state created after independence is perhaps the secret of the failure of African independence. (Cabral, 1973:84).

Nevertheless, the constant reference to the class foundations of the politics of national emancipation in particular throws up a contradiction expressed most clearly in Cabral's well-known remark concerning the need for the petty-bourgeoisie to 'commit class suicide' if it is not to betray the objectives of the struggle for national liberation:

> in order not to betray these objectives, the petty bourgeoisie has only one road: to strengthen its revolutionary consciousness, to repudiate the temptations to become 'bourgeois' and the natural pretentions of its class mentality; to identify with the classes of workers, not to oppose the normal development of the process of revolution. This means that... the revolutionary petty bourgeoisie must be capable of committing suicide as a class, to be restored to life in the condition of a revolutionary worker completely identified with the deepest aspirations of the people to which he belongs (Cabral, 1979:136).

The contradiction consists in the fact that, having insisted in historicist fashion that politics represents class interests, it becomes apparent to him that if emancipation is to be achieved especially after the moment of independence, class interests must be superseded by a politics largely in contradiction with class interests. Understanding this crucial problem however, Cabral is only able to express it in moral rather than political terms (Cabral, 1979: 136). The 'class suicide' of the petty bourgeoisie is made possible by its identification with popular cultures, in other words with a 'Return to the Source'. In the text reproduced below, the issue is treated in a more political and dialectical manner as the petty-bourgeoisie is understood as divided into three groups distinguished by their political relationship to the masses – to the *return to the source* – which is the final determinant of their commitment to national liberation. That *return to the source* is only historically (i.e. politically) important 'if it involves a genuine commitment to the fight for independence as well as a total, definitive identification with the aspirations of the popular masses'. As a result, the petty-bourgeoisie is divided between

> a) a minority which, even if it wishes the end of foreign rule, hangs on to the ruling colonial class, and openly opposes the movement in order to defend its social position;
> b) a majority of hesitant or undecided elements;
> c) another minority whose elements participate in creating and directing the liberation movement.

It thus follows for Cabral that 'culture then is decidedly not a weapon or a method of group mobilization against foreign domination. It is much more than that'. At the same time Cabral wants to create a new national identity that exceeds the parochial ethnic identities of the people which colonialism uses to divide and rule. Armed resistance must be seen as a prolongation of popular resistance against colonialism, and at the same time as an affirmation of the dignity of the people as Africans and full members of humanity.

> A reciprocal action develops between culture and the struggle. Culture, its foundation and source of inspiration, begins to be influenced by the struggle, and this influence is reflected more or less visibly in the evolving behaviour of social groups and individuals, as well as in the development of the struggle itself. Both the leaders of the liberation movement – mostly from ur-

ban centres (petty-bourgeoisie and wage earners) – and the popular masses, (overwhelmingly peasants) improve their cultural level. They increase their knowledge regarding the realities of their country, rid themselves of the complexes and prejudices of their class, overthrow the limits of their universe, destroy ethnic barriers, consolidate their political consciousness, integrate themselves more closely into their country and into the world, and so on.

Cabral's understanding that the state and the petty bourgeoisie who inherit state power can be an obstacle to freedom implies that his detailed dialectical thought of politics is able to push a historicist understanding to its limits. It could thus be suggested then that, even though Cabral's thought operates within a broadly historicist problematic, his immersion into thinking mass politics meant that he was never a complete prisoner of historicism. In brief Cabral's main political programme regarding popular culture is summed up in the following humanistic concerns:

> [...] in the perspective of developing the economic and social progress of the people, the objectives must be at least the following: development of a popular culture and of all positive indigenous cultural values; development of a national culture based upon the history and the achievements of the struggle itself; constant promotion of the political and moral awareness of the people (of all social groups) as well as patriotism, of the spirit of sacrifice and devotion to the cause of independence, of justice, and of progress; development of a technical, technological, and scientific culture, compatible with the requirements for progress; development, on the basis of a critical assimilation of man's achievements in the domains of art, science, literature, etc., of a universal culture for perfect integration into the contemporary world, in the perspectives of its evolution; constant and generalized promotion of feelings of humanism, of solidarity, of respect and disinterested devotion to human beings.
>
> The achievement of these objectives is indeed possible because the armed struggle for liberation, in the concrete condi-

tions of life of African peoples, confronted with the imperialist challenge, is an act of insemination upon history – the major expression of our culture and of our African essence. In the moment of victory, it must be translated into a significant leap forward of the culture of the people who are liberating themselves.

If that does not happen, then the efforts and sacrifices accepted during the struggle will have been made in vain. The struggle will have failed to achieve its objective and the people will have missed an opportunity for progress in the general framework of history (Cabral, 1973:55-56).

Unfortunately we know today that all the efforts and sacrifices accepted during the liberation struggle did not lead to the kind of popular power which Cabral was hoping for. Rather today we can say quite clearly that Africa's people are ruled by neocolonial states which have abandoned all attempts at rooting their institutions within popular cultures. It is this question which is explicitly addressed by Wamba-dia-Wamba.

Wamba-dia-Wamba: collective knowledge and the prescriptive quality of proverbs

It is possible to find in the twenty-first century today similar references to the emancipatory potential of African cultures. Yet these seem to be largely divorced from emancipatory politics for the most part (with rare exceptions).[5] Most people in the academy exhibit a tendency to think within the parameters of state discourses even when they attempt to take up positions critical of dominant Western paradigms. An exception here is to be found in the work of Ernest Wamba-dia-Wamba. For him thinking emancipation is no longer so much a question of the relationship between the party and the masses as was the case with Cabral. Rather than thinking in confrontation with the colonial state as in the twentieth century, it is now a question of thinking an emancipatory politics opposed to the neocolonial state as such. Political thought

---

[5] One exception in South Africa is the politics of Abahlali baseMjondolo, the Durban shackdweller's movement whose politics is very much located within traditional culture.

must therefore be developed at a distance from state modes of thought, and practice must be conceived outside the party form which is apparently an institution of this state through which individuals achieve power for their own narrow interests.

Central to this new conception of politics is a also a kind of *return to the source* by recovering the importance of the Mbongi and the Palaver, two village institutions which Wamba-dia-Wamba saw as central to the resolution of popular contradictions within communities. At the same time such traditional institutions are to enable the creation of a unified African alternative to the currently dominant Western conception of politics and democracy within the context of the Democratic Republic of Congo. His idea was to set up meetings, founded on this tradition, in Kinshasa itself in order to begin discussions among militants around what may be required to resist neocolonialism. The city-countryside distinction is still at the centre of Wamba-dia-Wamba's politics, but the city has largely become anomic as a result of having absorbed uncritically the Western conceptions that Cabral himself had warned against.

The problem: the African crisis

The central political problem overdetermining all others for Wamba-dia-Wamba is the neocolonial state in Africa which was historically simply grafted onto the colonial one at independence. He tells us that the 'state [...] has not developed organically with the African social body, rooted in, and imbued with African traditions and cultures'.

> Even political parties are grafts of the colonial masters' institutions which have not emerged organically from the social body of African society. As in medicine the social body tends to reject these transplants The crude characteristics of African political life can be explained on this basis. This is also the root of the crisis of the African state. We must also add to this the impact on the psychology (individual and social) and on the mentality of Africans of the slave trade, colonialism and racism.

The state must be restructured, he insists, so that it has a healthy relationship with the traditions, cultures and languages of the African peoples. What is needed is an elite organically linked to the community of the countryside, as well as to the urban community, and not a self-appointed communitarian elite representing the countryside for the interests of its individual members. The colonial state which has continued in only a slightly modified form after independence

> was a break between a communal rationality and a rationality of capitalist calculation. Instead of seeking a synthesis and continuity between the past, the present and the future, there developed a tabula rasa. The discontinuity between the past and the present has created a psychological situation characteristic of an urban mentality that consciously or unconsciously sought to annihilate the past associated with rural culture and the rural population.

We are told that this problem of discontinuity between traditional peasant culture and urban culture is fundamentally typical of Western modernity so that the failure to develop a synthesis between these two is at the root of what is experienced as an absence of meaning and depth in modern Western culture and its attendant personality. As a result we witness the 'ontological primacy of the individual over society, which reduces the latter to a meeting or contract between isolated individuals'. The consequences for African society of the imposition of this kind of state form on the colonized people and the subsequent grafting of the postcolonial state directly onto it had nefarious consequences.

> The profound meaning of dictatorship in Africa is the imposition of this graft on the whole of society, by means that aim at the violent and vicious destruction of peasant culture and traditions [...] The three African refusals can be explained on this basis: the refusal to think for oneself, the refusal to take seriously all of one's past and the refusal to see things in a long-term perspective. We speak with borrowed speeches, sometimes without being aware of it.

The solution: the Mbongi and the Palaver

Traditionally in Kongo villages, the Mbongi (also called Boko or Yemba) is a site around a fire where everyday experiences are exchanged.[6] Dominated by men but not exclusively so, 'the difficult intellectual work of mastering community struggles is undertaken at this site'. It is the basic deliberating and leading organ of the community. When experiences are exchanged, reference is often made to collective knowledge which is expressed as what the ancestors have said and takes the form of proverbs frequently metaphoric in form. Of course, different people may refer to different proverbs that the ancestors have expressed but as 'there is no quarrel about the character of the person who is quoting the ancestors because what is important is the truth of the statement, not the source or the person who utters it; and because we are not concerned with the subjectivity of the person, we can relate it to the ancestors because we all accept the ancestors' statements'. For Wamba-dia-Wamba proverbs are political prescriptions which affirm the unity of the community and its ontological primacy over individual being, as well as ensuring the reproduction of the community itself. Ontologically, first comes the multiplicity of the community from which follows that there is no such thing as an isolated individual. All individuals exist as products of the community of which they are a part. The collective multiplicity exists therefore prior to any individual.[7]

Because of this, knowledge is experienced as collectively produced in distinct particular circumstances. The fact that you can say 'the ancestors said this or that' is due to the fact that one is starting from traditions that have been accumulated over time. It follows that 'before you can say the new, you must state the old' which is uttered by reference to the proverbs emanating from the ancestors. If a major issue arises, for example someone has been caught doing something unacceptable, then the issue is brought to a palaver. The same is true of all communitarian non-antagonistic contradictions, in other words of differences between community members which may threaten the community itself, and also potentially antagonistic conflicts either within

---

[6] The following detailed information on the Mbongi and the Palaver is sourced predominantly from Wamba-dia-Wamba (forthcoming).

[7] The ontological primacy of the multiple as opposed to the 'one' which is here outlined in its African variant, acquires, in a different context, a detailed philosophical and mathematical enunciation in Alain Badiou (2005). The observant reader will notice the influence of Badiou's formulations on Ernest Wamba-dia-Wamba's arguments in several places below.

the community or with other communities. The palaver is then a meeting of the whole community called to address and to resolve a particular problem.

The process of the palaver is very complex and necessarily so, as it is a procedure to establish truth. It requires specific skilled people to guide it. These are the *Nzonzi*:

> To guide such a process, there are Nzonzi, specialists or elites from the community, sages, dialecticians (witnesses of the compossibility of community truths and detectors of bad speech, bad looks, etc.), lawyers, healers, community massagers, 'coolers' of the community bond in tension, rhetoricians or masters of public speaking, etc. [...] The palaver is not only the place of political processes that deal with matters of politics, that is to say the settlement of community relations, but it is also a place of participatory thought, in so far as thought is a relation to the real that the palaver requires.

In other words, the palaver is structured through rules that the *Kinzonzi* administer, and proverbs are cited so as to clarify issues and to maintain an 'ethics of truth'. The palaver for Wamba-dia-Wamba constitutes a new collective political site where contradictions among the people are resolved to everyone's satisfaction. The palaver is not concerned with establishing a consensus between different opinions. It is much more than that because its fundamental concern is to establish the truth of the situation, through a collective process in which all must participate without fear and speak in their own name. This process is accompanied by speeches, songs, poems, bodily gestures, theatrical expressions and the divisions of parties into 'commissions' within which all (even children) are encouraged to participate. Rhetoric is prized, but it is not prized for its own sake. The palaver is a democratic institution but not because it allows sophistry to proceed through rhetoric; it is concerned to establish the truth of the situation. Not all statements have the same value and many are false, and some actions are even considered evil such as individual accumulation at the expense of the community or failure to represent the community accurately. To put the point more metaphorically: 'a single mouth is an empty calabash'.

There is no form enforced a priori on a palaver. The character of the conflict being addressed determines the concrete form the palaver takes. It is not individuals who are judged in isolation, for any individual does not commit a crime but 'carries a crime'; the crime has its roots in the functioning of the community. Both have to be corrected; both must be healed. Finally, Wamba-dia-Wamba insists that the two most important values upheld by the Mbongi and the palaver and which ultimately guide its deliberations are the sanctity of the ancestral lands and the sovereignty of all human life.

Wamba-dia-Wamba concludes by observing that 'the grafted state, without any cultural roots, can only impose itself by force' much like the colonial state. Thus, his argument is reminiscent of Cabral's idea of a *return to the source*. The problem however is that, as Wamba recognizes, the Mbongi and the palaver are falling into disuse in the DRC as individual enrichment and class divisions force their way into the collective village community and people are fighting for state positions. For any process of renewal, *Kinzonzi* are required who understand tradition and the need to adapt it for the common good. All people must be involved in transforming social relations in society through a recognition of the importance of the old for establishing the new. The renewal of politics as a collective thought-practice must be founded on popular cultural practices in order to both heal society and produce new knowledge collectively, new truths from which popular political action can be informed and inform others.

Of course, in order to begin to think politically about transforming the neocolonial state which is simply a Western graft on a colonial foundation one has to insist on shifting to an African cultural understanding. But this understanding cannot be a spurious one created by power along the lines of Mobutu's Authenticité. Rather, what is required is precisely a turn to popular mass culture, the source of African traditions at least insofar as it has not been adulterated itself. It is a process of rediscovery which requires genuine political commitment. It is in a sense as Cabral put it, a genuine *return to the source*; not understood as a return to the past, but as a way of reconnecting with the old in order to construct the new. Popular traditions are then drawn upon as sources of knowledge in order to guide and enable the discovery of current truths. It is a manner of asserting that universal truths can be produced collectively through an understanding that a dialectical process rooted in cultural traditions can help reveal the universality of the human. As Wamba-dia-Wamba concludes, all this amounts to practicing the idea that people think.

Concluding Remarks

The difficulties encountered by the essentialist conceptions of ethnic culture created by dominant interests are well established. 'Tribalism' was seen as the curse of the postcolonial African state, particularly by those attempting to engage in some form of 'nation building'. It is well-known of course that the state power, from colonial domination onwards, systematically created or modified ethnicities in its interests. Overwhelmingly, this meant increasing the power of 'traditional authorities' over their subjects when these existed and creating them when they did not. This also meant developing, in various ways, a culture which enforced and eternalised ethnicities as fixed entities from which popular debates and consequently popularly devised changes were not simply discouraged but frequently excised altogether. The creation and manipulation of 'tribes' is the most well-known aspect of this process.[8] Yet, at the same time, popular cultural practices have not vanished, arguably because the reach of the state – legal, coercive and social – and the corresponding authoritarian interests of ethnic dominant groups, has never been total. The 'resurrection' of popular thought appears at intervals particularly during times of popular upsurge and resistance when cultural epistemics are drawn upon to enable precisely the kind of unity required to sustain popular movements and rebellions.

Both Cabral and Wamba-dia-Wamba refer to situations where popular cultures and debates had a significant amount of autonomy. Cabral's underestimation of or inability to handle adequately ethnic

---

[8] The literature is extensive but see inter alia L. Vail (1989), M. Mamdani (1996) and M. Neocosmos (2016).

contradictions in the PAIGC arguably led to his assassination.[9] For Ernest Wamba-dia-Wamba the subject of knowledge in African political thought is collective and not simply individual yet, at the same time, such collective thought is far removed from the mere conviviality of opinions (which ultimately encourages only sophistry) for it is a process of the becoming of a collective truth of the situation established through the activation of egalitarian and emancipatory potentials. These potentials need to be activated collectively in order to overcome popular contradictions – the first political step in achieving unity of purpose – because they exist mostly in a latent form in culture so that their emancipatory potential is not always evident. What tends to be apparent is rather their moral dimension. But an emancipatory politics, though grounded in morality, exceeds it because it is concerned with transforming society through a collective thought-practice which constructs political truths through discussion and debate. And it does so within a present informed by the accumulated experiences and emancipatory experiments of our ancestors. This is why the concepts of the past must, through collective activation, be given new meaning in the present so that they become fully of the present, and do not simply exist today as remnants and museum pieces to be idealised by a constructed ethnic revivalism.

---

[9] See António Tomás (2021) who discusses the main ethno-national divisions within the liberation movement of Guinea and his difficulty in producing a national unity especially between Cape Verdians and Guineans. The universalism of Cabral's thought was it seems always contested from within his movement.

References

Badiou, A. (2005) Being and Event, London: Continuuum.

Cabral, A. (1973) Return to the Source, New York: Monthly Review Press.

Cabral, A. (1979) Unity and Struggle, Speeches and Writings, New York: Monthly Review Press

Gordon, L. (2008) Introduction to Africana Philosophy, Cambridge University Press

Mamdani, M. (1996) Citizen and Subject, Oxford: James Currey.

Neocosmos, M. (2016a) 'The Politics of National Emancipation in Africa: subversive thought in Cabral's Resistance and Decolonization', Theory and Event, Special Issue 19.4. October.

Neocosmos, M. (2016b) Thinking Freedom in Africa, Jo'burg: Wits University Press.

Sekyi-Otu, A. (2018) Left Universalism, Africacentric essays, London: Routledge

Tomás, A. (2021) Amílcar Cabral: the life of a reluctant nationalist, London: Hurst and Co.

Vail, L. (ed.) (1989) The Creation of Tradition in Southern Africa, London: James Currey.

Wamba-dia-Wamba, E. 'Experiences of Democracy in Africa: Reflections on Practices of Communalist Palaver as a Social Method of Resolving Contradictions among the People', Philosophy and Social Action XI (3) 1985. See also https://www.newframe.com/archive-communalist-palaver/ accessed 01/11/2021 Also available in M. Neocosmos (ed.) An Anthology of African Political Thought from Ancient Egypt to the Present, Dakar: Codesria forthcoming.

Wamba-dia-Wamba, E. (forthcoming) The Thought and Practice of an Emancipatory Politics for Africa by Wamba-dia-Wamba publication forthcoming Tricontinental Institute of Social Research, Johannesburg.

The role of culture in the struggle for independence[10]

Amílcar Cabral

Preamble

Only the desire to accept UNESCO's kind invitation and a deep conviction of the importance of the topic proposed have made me feel able to work on this little paper at a time when obligations to my people, in their hard struggle for independence, require that I devote my every moment to the study and solution of national problems.

Rather than cover all the various points suggested, I have concentrated on the importance of culture in a pre-independence or liberation movement. Since there has obviously not been time to go to the book and documentary sources which would doubtless have given this paper a broader foundation and richer substance, I have practically confined myself to presenting the fruit of my own experience to what I have observed, both in our own struggle against imperialist rule and as a student of other struggles. In the section dealing specifically with the role of culture in the liberation movement, I have developed ideas and re-

---

[10] This speech was originally written in French as *Sur le role de la culture dans la lutte pour l'indépendance*. It was delivered at the UNESCO Meeting of Experts on Questions of Race, Identity, and Dignity, Paris, 3-7 July 1972, in the absence of its author. The text below is based on the official UNESCO translation. Editorial changes have been kept to a minimum and have been introduced for greater clarity and with reference to the original French text. Source: UNESCO https://unesdoc.unesco.org/ark:/48223/pf0000001749 accessed 20/07/2021

flections contained in a lecture I gave at Syracuse University (United States of America) in February 1970 on 'National Liberation and Culture'.[11] Because of the conditions under which it was written and the limitations of my knowledge, the paper has shortcomings which the generous reader will, if not excuse, at least understand. But if I succeed in convincing him of the crucial importance of culture in the development of the liberation movement, or in strengthening his conviction, this work would not have been in vain.

Introduction

The struggle of peoples for national liberation and independence against imperialist rule has become an immense progressive force for human progress and is beyond doubt an essential feature of the history of our time.

An objective analysis of imperialism as a *fact* or historical *phenomenon* that is 'natural', even 'necessary' to the economic and political evolution of a great part of mankind, reveals that imperialist rule with its train of miseries, pillage, crimes, and destruction of human and cultural values was not a purely negative reality. The huge accumulation of capital by a half-dozen countries of the northern hemisphere as a result of piracy, of the pillage of other people's property, and unbridled exploitation of their labour did more than engender colonial monopoly, the partition of the world, and imperialist domination.

In the wealthy countries, imperialist capital, ever looking for higher profits, heightened man's creative capacity; it profoundly transformed the means of production through the accelerated progress of science, techniques, and technology; it increased the socialization of labour; and it enabled vast strata of the population to be upwardly mobile. In the colonized countries, where colonization usually arrested the development of the colonized peoples – when it did not just wipe them out altogether or bit by bit – imperialist capital imposed new types of relationships within native society whose structure became more complex. It instigated, fomented, inflamed, or resolved social

---

[11] Editor's note: see A. Cabral 'National Liberation and Culture' in Return to the Source: selected speeches of Amílcar Cabral, New York: Monthly Review Press, 1973 pp.39-56.

contradictions and conflicts. It introduced new elements into the economy through the circulation of money and the development of domestic and foreign trade. It led to the birth of new nations based out of human groups or peoples at varying stages of historical development.

It is not to defend imperialist rule to recognize that, by reducing the world's dimensions, it gave it new worlds; that it revealed new phases in the development of human societies, and, in spite of or because of the prejudices, the discrimination and the crimes it occasioned, it helped to impart a deeper knowledge of mankind, as a whole in movement, as a *unit* in the complex, diverse characteristics of its development.

On different continents imperialist rule fostered a multilateral, gradual (sometimes abrupt) confrontation not only between different men but between different societies. The practice of imperialist rule – its affirmation or its negation – required (and still requires) a more or less accurate knowledge of the *dominated object* and the historical reality (economic, social, and cultural) within which it moves, this knowledge necessarily being expressed in terms of comparison with the *dominating subject* and *its* historical reality. Such knowledge is an imperative necessity for the practice of imperialist rule, which usually results from the violent confrontation of two *identities* distinct in their historical content and antagonistic in their functions. The quest for such knowledge contributed to a general enrichment of the human and social sciences, despite its being unilateral, subjective, and very often unjust.

Man has never taken such an interest in knowing other men and other societies as during this century of imperialist domination. Thus, an unprecedented amount of information, hypotheses and theories accumulated – especially in the fields of history, ethnology, ethnography, sociology, and culture – regarding the subjugated peoples and human groups. Concepts of race, caste, ethnicity, tribe, nation, culture, identity, dignity, and so many again have received growing attention from those who study man and so-called 'primitive' or 'developing' societies.

More recently, with the upsurge of liberation movements, it has been found necessary to analyse the characteristics of these societies in terms of the struggle that is being fought to determine the factors that touch it off or restrain it. Research workers generally agree that in this context culture takes on a particular importance. It can be accepted then that any attempt to throw light on the true role of culture in the development of a liberation (pre-independence) movement can make a helpful contribution to the general struggle of peoples against imperialist rule.

I

Because independence movements are generally marked, even at their early phase, by a succession of demonstrations of a cultural character, it is taken for granted that these have been preceded by a 'cultural renaissance' of the dominated people. This view is taken even further to suggest that culture is a method of group mobilization and even a *weapon* in the fight for independence.

From experience of our own struggle and it could be said that of all of Africa, I feel that this amounts to a too limited, if not erroneous, conception of the vital role of culture in the development of the liberation movement. I think this view comes from an incorrect generalizing of a real but restricted phenomenon that appears at a particular level of the vertical structure of colonized societies – the level of colonial *elites* or *diasporas*. Such generalizing exhibits an ignorance or neglect of an essential datum of the problem: the indestructible character of cultural resistance by the popular masses to foreign rule.

To be sure, the exercise of imperialist domination demands cultural oppression and the attempt at direct or indirect liquidation of what is essential in the culture of the dominated people. But the latter is only able to create and develop the liberation movement because it keeps its culture alive in the teeth of the permanent and organised repression of its cultural life – only because, its politico-military resistance having been destroyed, it continues to resist culturally. And it is this cultural resistance which, at a given moment, may take on new forms (political, economic, armed) in order to contest foreign domination.

With a few exceptions, the *era of colonization* was not of sufficient length, in Africa at least, to destroy or significantly depreciate the essential elements in the culture and traditions of the colonized people. The colonial experience of imperialist domination in Africa shows that (genocide, racial segregation and 'apartheid' excepted) the only allegedly 'positive' way the colonial power has found for opposing cultural resistance is 'assimilation'. But the total failure of the policy of 'gradual assimilation' of native populations is the obvious proof both of the fallacy of the theory and of peoples' capacity for resistance.[12] On the other hand, even in settler colonies, where the overwhelming majority of the population is still indigenous, the area of colonial occupation and particularly that of *cultural occupation*, is usually restricted to coastal strips and to a few limited areas in the interior. The influence of the colonial power's culture is almost nil beyond the bounds of the capital and other urban centres. It is felt significantly only at the apex of the social pyramid – that which colonialism itself created – and especially affects what may be called the 'indigenous petty-bourgeoisie' and a very limited number of workers in urban centres.

We find then that the great rural masses, and a large fraction of the urban population – making up a total of over 99 percent of the native population – remain apart, or almost so, from any cultural influence of the colonial power. This situation derives on the one hand from the necessarily obscurantist character of imperialist rule which, while despising and repressing the culture of the dominated people, has little interest in promoting the acculturation of the popular masses, the source of forced-labour and the prime object of exploitation. On the other hand, it derives from the effective cultural resistance of those masses who, subjected to political rule and to economic exploitation, find in their own culture the one bulwark strong enough to preserve their *identity*. Where the indigenous society has a vertical structure, this defence of its cultural heritage is further reinforced by the colonial power's interest in protecting and strengthening the cultural influence of that society's dominant classes which are its allies.

What I have said suggests that, not only for the popular masses in the dominated country but also for the dominant classes among the indigenous peoples (traditional chiefs, noble families, religious authorities), there is usually no destruction or significant degradation of culture and traditions. Repressed, persecuted, humiliated, and betrayed by various social groups that have come to terms with the foreigner, taking refuge in the villages, in forests, and in the minds of the victims of domination, culture weathers every storm to recover, through the struggle for liberation, all its powers of expansion. That is why the

---

[12] Insofar as the Portuguese colonies are concerned, the largest percentage of assimilated persons is 0.3 percent of the total population (in Guinea) after five hundred years of a civilizing presence and a half-century of 'colonial peace'.

problem of a 'return to the source' or a 'cultural renaissance' does not arise nor could it for the popular masses; it could not, for the masses are the bearers of culture, they are themselves its source, and at the same time, the only entity truly capable of preserving and creating this culture, of *making history*.

In order to acquire a correct appreciation of the true role of culture in the development of the liberation movement, a distinction must therefore be made, at least in Africa, between the situation of the masses who preserve their culture, and that of the social groups which are more or less assimilated, uprooted, and culturally alienated. Even though they may bear certain cultural features belonging to the native community, indigenous elites, themselves created by the colonizing process, live materially and spiritually the culture of the colonialist foreigner with whom they seek gradually to identify themselves in social behaviour and even in their view of indigenous cultural values.

Over two or three generations of colonization at least, a social stratum has been formed composed of government officials, employees in various branches of the economy (particularly trade), members of liberal professions, and a few urban and agricultural proprietors. This indigenous petty-bourgeoisie, created by foreign rule and indispensable to the system of colonial exploitation, is located between the popular masses of rural and urban labour and the minority of local representatives of the foreign ruling class. Although its members may have, more or less extensive relations with the popular masses or with traditional chiefs, they usually aspire to a way of life similar to, if not identical with, that of the foreign minority. They limit their intercourse with the masses and at the same time try to become integrated into that minority, often to the detriment of family or ethnic bonds and always at personal cost. But whatever the apparent exceptions, they do not succeed in crossing the barriers imposed by the system. They are prisoners of the contradictions of the social and cultural reality within which they live, for they cannot escape, under a 'colonial peace', their condition as a *marginal* or 'marginalized' class. Both *locally* and within the diasporas implanted in the colonial metropolis, this 'marginality' constitutes the socio-cultural drama of the colonised elites or native 'petty-bourgeoisie', a drama lived more or less intensely according to material conditions and levels of acculturation, but always at the individual and not the community level.

Within the framework of this daily drama, against the background of the usually violent confrontation between the popular masses and the colonial ruling class, a feeling of bitterness or a *frustration complex* develops and grows among the indigenous petty-bourgeoisie. Along with this, they become conscious little by little of an urgent need to contest their marginal status and to discover an *identity* for themselves. So they turn towards the other pole of the socio-cultural conflict in which they are living – the native masses. Hence the 'return to the source' which seems all the more imperative as the isolation of the petty-bourgeoisie (or native elites) grows, and as its sense of frustration becomes acute – as is also the case among the African diasporas implanted in colonial or racist metropoles. It is not by chance then that theories or movements such as Pan-Africanism and Negritude – two pertinent expressions based mainly on the postulate that all Black Africans are culturally identical – were conceived outside Black Africa. More recently, the Black Americans' claim to an African identity is another manifestation, perhaps desperate, of this need to 'return to the source', though clearly influenced by a new fact: the winning of political independence by the great majority of African peoples.

But a 'return to the source' neither is nor can be, in itself, an *act of struggle* against foreign rule (colonialist and racist), nor does it necessarily mean a return to tradition. Needing to identify with the subject people, the indigenous petty-bourgeoisie deny that the culture of the ruling power is superior to theirs, as claimed. A 'return to the source' then is not a voluntary step, but rather the only viable response to the powerful pressure of a concrete historical necessity determined by the irreducible opposition – colonized society versus colonial power, exploited masses versus foreign exploiting class – in relation to which every indigenous social stratum or class is obliged to define its position.

When the 'return to the source' extends beyond the individual and expresses itself in 'groups' or 'movements', this opposition turns into a conflict (concealed or open) which is the prelude to the movement of independence or struggle for liberation from the foreign yoke. This 'return to the source' is historically important only if it involves a genuine commitment to the fight for independence as well as a total, definitive identification with the aspirations of the popular masses who contest not merely the foreigners' culture but foreign rule altogether.

Otherwise, a 'return to the source' is nothing but a means of obtaining temporary advantages, a conscious or unconscious form of political opportunism.

It must be pointed out that a 'return to the source', whether seeming or real, is not something that happens simultaneously and uniformly within the native petty-bourgeoisie. It is a slow, discontinuous, uneven process the development of which depends on each person's degree of acculturation, the material conditions of his life, his ideological training, and his own history as a social being. This unevenness is the basis for the splitting of the indigenous petty-bourgeoisie into three groups in the face of the liberation movement:

(a) A minority which, even if it wishes the end of foreign rule, hangs on to the ruling colonial class, and openly opposes the movement in order to defend its social position;

(b) A majority of hesitant or undecided elements;

(c) Another minority whose elements participate in creating and directing the liberation movement.

But this last group, which plays a decisive role in developing the pre-independence movement does not really succeed in identifying itself with the popular masses (their culture, their aspirations) except through the struggle, the degree of identification depending on the form or forms of the struggle, the ideological content of the movement and the level of each man's moral and political awareness.

II

For a part of the native petty-bourgeoisie to identify with the popular masses presupposes one essential condition: *that against the destructive action of imperialist domination, the masses preserve their identity*, different and distinct from that of the colonial power. So it seems important to determine in which cases this preservation is possible; why, when and at what levels of the subject society the problem of loss, or lack of identity arises, making it necessary to assert or reassert in the framework of the pre-independence movement, a different distinct identity.

The identity of a given individual or human group is a bio-sociological quality, independent of the will of this individual or group, but meaningful only when expressed in relation to other ones. The dialectical nature of identity lies in the fact that identity *identifies* and distinguishes, for an individual (or human group) is identical with certain individuals (or groups) only if distinct from other ones. The definition of an individual or collective identity, therefore, is at once the affirmation and the negation of a certain number of characteristics defining individuals or communities in terms of *historical,* biological and sociological coordinates at one moment in their evolution. Identity is not an immutable quality for the very reason that the biological and sociological data that define it are in constant evolution. Biologically or sociologically, there are in time no two beings (individual or collective) absolutely identical or absolutely distinct, for it is always possible to find distinguishing or identifying characteristics. So, the identity of a being is always a relative and indeed a circumstantial feature, for its definition requires a fairly rigorous, or restricted selection of the being's biological and sociological characteristics.

It must be observed that in the fundamental binomial which the definition of identity represents, the sociological is more determinant than the biological. While it is true that the biological element (the genetic heritage) is the indispensable material basis for the existence of evolutionary continuity of identity, the fact remains that the sociological element is the factor which, by giving this quality content and form, gives it objective significance and makes it possible to confront or compare individuals or groups of individuals. Indeed, to arrive at the integral definition of identity, characterization of the biological element is indispensable, but does not imply an identification on the sociological plane, whereas two sociologically identical beings have necessarily a similar identity on the biological plane.

This fact shows on the one hand, the supremacy of social life over individual life, for society (human, for example) is a higher form of life. On the other hand, it suggests that in appreciating identity, we must not confuse original identity, in which the biological element is the chief determinant, with current identity in which the chief determinant is the sociological element. Obviously, the identity to be reckoned with at any given moment, in the evolution of a being (individual or collective), is current identity, and any appreciation based solely on original identity is incomplete, partial, and fallacious for it neglects or is ignorant of the decisive influence of social reality on the content and form of identity.

In the formation and development of individual or community identity, social reality is an objective agent resulting from the economic, political, social, and cultural factors that characterize the society's evolution or history. If we consider that among these factors the economic is fundamental, we can say that identity is in some sense, the expression of an economic fact. Whatever the society's geographic setting and line of development, this reality is defined by the level of productive powers (the relations between men and nature) and the mode of production (relations between men or groups of men within one society). But if we grant that culture is the dynamic synthesis of the society's material and spiritual reality and expresses both relations between men and nature and relations between different groups of men in one society, we may say that identity, at individual or community level and above and beyond economic facts, is the expression of a culture. That is why to assign, to recognize, or to assert the identity of an individual or human group is above all to situate the individual or group within the framework of a culture. Now, as everyone knows, the chief support of culture in every society is the social structure. It then seems reasonable to conclude that for any given human group, the possibility of preserving (or losing) its identity in the face of foreign rule, depends on how far that rule has destroyed its social structure.

Concerning the effects of imperialist domination on the social structure of a dominated people, it is essential to consider the case of classical colonialism, which is what the pre-independence movement is contesting. In this case, irrespective of the stage of historical development of the dominated society, its social structure may suffer the following effects:

1. *Total destruction*, along with the immediate or gradual liquidation of the indigenous population, and its replacement by an exotic one.

2. *Partial destruction*, along with the establishment of a more or less numerous exotic population.

3. *Apparent conservation*, conditioned by confinement of the indigenous society to geographic zones or reserves, usually lacking the conditions of life, along with the massive implantation of an exotic population.

The essentially horizontal character of African peoples' social structure due to the profusion of ethnic groups, means that cultural resistance and the degree of preservation of identity are not uniform. Thus, while it is true that, in general, ethnic groups have succeeded in keeping their identity, we find that the groups that *resist* the most are the ones that have had the most violent clashes with the colonial power during the phase of effective occupations[13] or those that, through geographical isolation, have been least in contact with the foreign presence.[14] It must be observed that the attitude of the colonial power towards ethnic groups is hopelessly contradictory. On the one hand this power must divide or maintain divisions in order to rule and therefore, it encourages separation, if not quarrels between ethnic groups. On the other hand, in trying to ensure the perpetuation of its rule, it has to destroy the social structure, the culture and the identity of those groups. Moreover, it is forced to defend the governing classes of groups, which like the Fulani (*Peulh*) people or nation in my country for instance, gave it decisive support at the time of colonial conquest, a policy which tends to preserve the identity of those groups.

As I have already said, as regards culture, there are usually no important cultural modifications within the hierarchy of the indigenous social pyramid or pyramids (groups or societies which possess a state). Each stratum or class keeps its identity integrated in that of the group, but distinct from the identities of other social groups. By contrast, in urban centres and in certain zones of the interior of the country where the colonial power's cultural influence is felt, the problem of identity is more complex. Whereas those at the base of the social pyramid (that is the majority of the labouring popular masses made up of individuals from different ethnic groups) and those at the summit (the foreign ruling class) preserve their identities, those in the middle zone of this pyramid (the native petty-bourgeoisie) – culturally rootless, alienated, or more or less assimilated – flounder in a social and cultural conflict in quest of their identity. It must also be pointed out that while united by a new identity – conferred on it by the colonial power – the foreign ruling class does not succeed in freeing itself from the contradictions of its own society which it imports.

---

[13] In my country the Mandjaks, Pepels, Oincas, Balantes, and Beafadas.

[14] This is the case with the Pajadincas and other minorities in the interior.

When the pre-independence movement gets underway on the initiative of a minority of the native petty-bourgeoisie in alliance with the indigenous masses, these masses have no need to assert or reassert their identity; they could never possibly have confused it with that of the colonial power. This need is felt only by the native petty-bourgeois who are forced to take a stand in the conflict opposing the popular masses to the colonial power. But the reassertion of an identity distinct from that of the colonial power, is not the general case among the petty-bourgeoisie. It is only made by a minority whereas another asserts, often noisily, its identity with the foreign ruling class, while the silent majority dithers, indecisive.

Besides, even when there is reassertion of an identity distinct from that of the colonial power's and therefore the same as that of the masses, it is not manifested in the same way everywhere. Part of the petty-bourgeois minority engaged in the pre-independence movement makes use of foreign culture, drawing especially on literature and the arts to express the discovery of their own identity, rather than the aspirations and sufferings of the popular masses that serve as their artistic themes. And just because they use the language and speech of the colonial power, they can only very exceptionally influence the popular masses who are mostly illiterate and familiar with other forms of artistic expression. Still, that does not diminish the value of the contribution of this petty-bourgeois minority to the development of the struggle, for they succeeded all the same in influencing some of the indecisive, or backward elements of their own social group as well as a large section of public opinion in the colonial metropolis, particularly intellectuals. The other part of the petty-bourgeoisie, engaged in the pre-independence movement *from the very beginning*, find immediate participation in the liberation struggle and integration with the masses the best way of expressing an identity distinct from that of the colonial power.

That is why identification with the masses and the reassertion of identity may be temporary or permanent, apparent or real in the face of the day-to-day efforts and sacrifices demanded by the struggle itself; a struggle which, even though it is the organized political expression of a *culture*, is also necessarily a proof, not solely of *identity*, but also of *dignity*.

Throughout the process of colonial rule, the popular masses, irrespective of the social structure of the group to which they belong, continue to resist the colonial power. In a first phase – during the colonial conquest cynically labelled 'pacification' – they resist foreign occupation weapons in hand. In a second phase – the golden age of triumphant colonialism – they offer resistance that is passive, almost silent, but interspersed by many rebellions (usually individual and rarely collective) particularly in the areas of work, concerning taxation, and even regarding social contacts with foreign or indigenous representatives of the colonial power. In a third phase – the struggle for liberation – it is they who furnish the main force for political or armed resistance, for contesting and liquidating foreign rule. Such resistance, prolonged and multiform, is only possible because, by preserving their culture and their identity, the masses keep the consciousness of their individual and community dignity intact despite the vexations, humiliations, and cruelties they are often exposed to.

The assertion or reassertion by the indigenous petty-bourgeoisie of an identity distinct from that of the colonial power does not and cannot help to restore a sense of dignity to this single social group. Still in this context, it must be observed that, the sense of dignity of the petty-bourgeoisie depends on each person's objectively moral and social behaviour, and on how far he is subjective in his attitude towards the two poles of the social conflict between which he has to live out the day-to-day drama of colonization. This drama is all the more intense in that in discharging their functions, the petty-bourgeoisie is forced into continual contact, both with the ruling foreigners and with the popular masses. So, on the one hand they suffer frequent if not daily humiliation at the hands of the foreigner and on the other, they become aware of the injustices inflicted on the masses, and of the latter's resistance and rebellious spirit. Hence, we observe a paradox in the challenge to colonial rule: it is directly within the native petty-bourgeoisie, a social category created by colonialism itself, that there appear the first important initiatives aimed at mobilizing and organizing the popular masses for the struggle against the colonial power. Through all vicissitudes and regardless of its forms, this struggle reflects an awareness, or the birth of an awareness of a specific identity; it generalizes and consolidates a sense of dignity reinforced by the development of political consciousness, and it draws from the culture or cultures of the rebellious masses one of its main sources of strength.

III

A correct appreciation of what culture means in the pre-independence movement requires that a clear distinction be made between *culture* and *cultural demonstrations*. Culture is the dynamic synthesis at the level of individual or community consciousness of the material and spiritual historical reality of a society or a human group of the relations existing between men and nature, as well as among men and among social groupings. Cultural demonstrations are the various forms through which this synthesis is expressed individually or collectively at each stage in the evolution of this society or group.

Culture has proved to be the very foundation of the liberation movement. Mobilization, organization, and struggle against foreign rule have proved possible only for societies that preserve their culture. Whatever the ideological or idealistic characteristics of its expression may be, culture is an essential element of the historical process. It is culture that has the capacity for elaborating, or fertilizing elements which ensure the historical continuity of the society, at the same time determining its possibilities of social progress, or regression. Thus, it will be understood that as imperialist rule is the negation of the historical process of the dominated society, it is necessarily the negation of its cultural process. Because a society that truly liberates itself from the foreign yoke returns to the upward paths of its own culture, which is nourished by the living reality of the environment and rejects baneful influences, and any kind of subjection to foreign cultures, it follows that the struggle for liberation is, before all else, *an act of culture*.

The fight for liberation is an essential political fact. Consequently, as it develops, it can only use political methods (including violence to end the armed violence, of imperialist rule). Culture then is decidedly not a weapon or a method of group mobilization against foreign domination. It is much more than that. Indeed, it is from within a concrete knowledge of local reality, particularly of cultural reality that the choice, the structure, and the development of the most adequate methods of fighting, are founded. Therefore, the liberation struggle must accord primary importance not only to the cultural characteristics of the dominated society in general, but also to those of each social grouping. For, although it exhibits a mass character, culture is not uniform; it is not evenly developed in all sectors of society, whether horizontal [mainly ethnic] or vertical [hierarchical].

The attitudes and behaviour of each category or of each individual towards the struggle and its unfolding are certainly dictated by economic interests, but are also profoundly influenced by culture. It may even be said that the difference of cultural level is what explains differences in behaviour among individuals in the same social category, towards the liberation movement. It is on this plane then that culture attains its full significance for every person: comprehension of and integration in his social milieu, identification with the fundamental problems and aspirations of his society, acceptance or rejection of the possibility of progressive change.

Clearly, a multiplicity of social groups, particularly ethnic ones, makes the role of culture in the liberation movement more difficult to define, but this complexity cannot and must not lessen the decisive importance to the movement of the *class character* of culture, which is more evident in urban groupings and rural societies with a vertical structure, and should be considered, even when the phenomenon of class is embryonic. Experience shows that when the revolt against foreign rule forces them to make a political choice, most members of the privileged groups put their immediate class interests above the interests of their group in society, against the aspirations of the popular masses.

Nor must we forget that culture as a cause as well as an effect of history, includes essential and secondary elements, strengths and weaknesses merits and defects, positive and negative aspects, factors for progress or for stagnation or regression, contradictions and even conflicts. However complex this cultural panorama may be, the liberation movement must recognize and define this contradictory data, so as to protect the positive values and *channel* them in the direction of the struggle with an added dimension: the *national dimension*. But it must be observed that it is only when the struggle is actually underway that the complexity and importance of these cultural problems become fully apparent; so that often there have to be successive adaptations of strategy and tactics to the realities which the struggle alone can reveal. Moreover, only the struggle can show what an inexhaustible source of courage, culture is for the popular masses, what a source of physical and psychic energy it is, but also what a source of obstacles and difficulties, erroneous conceptions, deviations in fulfilment of duties and limitations of the rhythm and efficacy of the struggle it can be.

All this implies a permanent confrontation both between different elements of the culture, and between the culture and the demands of the struggle. A reciprocal action develops between culture and the struggle. Culture, its foundation and source of inspiration, begins to be influenced by the struggle, and this influence is reflected more or less visibly in the evolving behaviour of social groups and individuals, as well as in the development of the struggle itself. Both the leaders of the liberation movement – mostly from urban centres (petty-bourgeoisie and wage earners) – and the popular masses, (overwhelmingly peasants) improve their cultural level. They increase their knowledge regarding the realities of their country, rid themselves of the complexes and prejudices of their class, overthrow the limits of their universe, destroy ethnic barriers, consolidate their political consciousness, integrate themselves more closely into their country and into the world, and so on.

Whatever its form, we know that the struggle requires the mobilization and organization of a large majority of the population, the political and moral unity of different social groupings, the gradual elimination of vestiges of tribal and feudal mentalities, and the rejection of social and religious taboos incompatible with the *rational* and national character of the liberation movement and the struggle brings about many other profound modifications in the life of the population. This is all the more true because the dynamic of the struggle also requires the exercise of democracy, criticism and self-criticism, the growing participation by populations in running their lives, literacy, the creation of schools and health services, leadership training for cadres from rural or urban labouring backgrounds, and many other achievements that impel society to set forth upon the road of cultural progress. This shows that the liberation struggle is not solely a cultural fact, it is also a *cultural factor* [i.e. a producer of culture].

Within indigenous society, the action of the liberation movement on the cultural plane entails the creation of a slow but solid cultural unity, symbiotic in nature, corresponding to the moral and political unity necessary to the dynamic of the struggle. With the opening-up of hermetic groups, tribal or ethnic racist aggressiveness tends gradually to disappear and give way to understanding, to solidarity and to mutual respect among the various horizontal sectors of society, united in struggle and in a common destiny in the face of foreign rule. These are sentiments which the popular masses imbibes readily enough if the process is not hindered by the political opportunism peculiar to the middle classes. It can also be observed that group identity and, as a consequence, a sense of dignity are both reinforced. All this serves the movement of society as a whole towards harmonious progress in terms of the new historical co-ordinates. Only intensive effective political action, the essential element in the struggle, can define the trajectory and bounds of this movement, and ensure its continuity.

Among representatives of the colonial power, as in metropolitan opinion, the first reaction to the liberation struggle is a general feeling of amazement and incredulity. Once this feeling, the fruit of prejudice or of the planned distortion that typifies colonialist news is surmounted, reactions vary with the interests, the political options, and the degree of crystallization of a colonialist or racist mentality among the different social sectors, even among individuals. The progress of the struggle and the sacrifices imposed by the need to exert colonial repression, whether police or military, cause a split in metropolitan opinion; this is expressed in differing if not divergent positions and new political and social contradictions emerge.

From the moment when the struggle has asserts itself as an irreversible fact, no matter how much may be done to strangle it, a qualitative change takes place in metropolitan opinion. On the whole, the possibility if not the inevitability of the colony's independence is gradually accepted. Such a change expresses a conscious or unconscious admission of the fact that the colonized people now in struggle, have an identity and a culture of their own; and this despite the fact that an active minority clinging to its interest and prejudices throughout the conflict, persists in refusing them their right to independence, and in rejecting the equivalence of cultures, which that right implies. At a decisive stage in the conflict, this equivalence is implicitly recognized or accepted even by the colonial power but in order to divert the struggle from its objectives, it applies a demagogic policy of 'economic and social promotion' of 'cultural development', having recourse to domination in new forms. Actually, if neocolonialism is above all the continuation of imperialist economic rule in disguise, it is also the tacit recognition by the colonial power that the people it rules and exploits has an identity of its own that demands its own political direction for the satisfaction of a necessary cultural requirement.

It must further be observed that by accepting the existence of an identity, and a culture among the colonized people, and therefore its inalienable right to self-determination and independence, metropolitan opinion (or at least an important part of it) itself makes significant cultural progress and sheds a negative element in its own culture: the prejudice that the colonizing nation is superior to the colonized one. This advance may have important – transcendental – consequences for the political evolution of the imperialist or colonial power, as is proved by certain facts of recent or current history.

Certain genetico-somatic and cultural affinities between several human groups on one or more continents, and a more or less similar situation regarding colonial or racist domination, have led to the formulation of theories, and the creation of 'movements' based on the hypothetical existence of *racial* or *continental cultures*. The importance of culture in the liberation movement, widely recognized or sensed, has helped to give this hypothesis a certain following. While the importance of such theories or movements as attempts, successful or not, at seeking an identity, and as a means of contesting foreign rule should not be minimized, it can be maintained that an objective analysis of cultural reality leads to the denial of the existence of racial or continental cultures. First, because culture like history is an expanding phenomenon and closely linked to the economic and social reality of its milieu, and to the level of the productive powers and the mode of production of the society that created it. Second, because culture develops unevenly at the level of a continent or a 'race', or even of a community. In fact, the coordinates of culture, like those of every other developing phenomenon, vary in space and time, whether they are material (physical) or human (biological and sociological). That is why culture – the creation of a society and the synthesis of balances and solutions it engenders in order to resolve the contradictions that confront it at every phase of its history – is a social reality, independent of men's will, the colour of their skin, the shape of their eyes, or of their geographical location.

A correct appreciation of the role of culture in the liberation movement requires that we consider its defining factors as a whole and in their internal relations; that we avoid any confusion between what is the expression of a historical material reality and that which seems to be a creation of the mind, detached from that reality; that we do not set up an absurd connection between artistic creations whether valuable or not, and the so-called psychic and somatic characteristics of a 'race'; and finally, that we avoid any non-scientific or a-scientific analysis of the phenomenon of culture.

For culture to play its due part within it, the liberation movement must establish the precise objectives to be achieved on the way towards reconquering the rights of the people it represents and leads towards the making its own history, and towards achieving the free disposal of its own productive powers with an end to the eventual development of a richer culture – popular, national, scientific and universal. What is important for the liberation movement is not to prove the specificity or non-specificity of the people's culture, but to analyse it critically in the light of the requirements of the struggle and of progress; to give it its place, without either a superiority or an inferiority complex, within universal civilization as a part of the common heritage of mankind, with a view to a harmonious integration into the present-day world.

The liberation struggle which is the most complex expression of the people's cultural vigour, of its identity and of its dignity, enriches culture and opens up new prospects for its development. Cultural demonstrations acquire a new content and find new forms of expression. Thus, they become a powerful instrument of political information and training, not only in the struggle for independence, but also in the great battle for progress.

Bibliography

Berghe, Pierre, L. v d (1971) 'L'ethnicité en Afrique' *Revue internationale des sciences sociales*, XXIII no 4, pp.551-569.

Beteille, A. (1971) 'Race, caste et identité ethnique', *Revue internationale des sciences sociales*, XXIII, No.4 pp.551-569.

Cabral, A. (1969) *Revolution in Guinea*, New York: Monthly Review Press.

Cabral, A. (1973) 'National Liberation and Culture' in *Return to the Source: selected speeches of Amílcar Cabral*, New York: Monthly Review Press, 1973 pp.39-56.

Davidson, B. (1969) The African Genius, Boston and Toronto: Little Brown.

Kuper, L. (1971) 'Le changement d'ordre politique dans les sociétés pluralists: problems poses par le pluralism racial' *Revue international des sciences sociales,* XXIII No.4, pp.632-645.'

The *Mbongi* and the *Palaver* yesterday, today and tomorrow

Ernest Wamba-dia-Wamba

Kinshasa, 18 October 2003, first meeting of the *Mbongi A Nsi*[15]

Have our cultures ceased to be able to deal with conflicts and contradictions among the people? Why does the dialectic of the articulation of roots and wings not yet give the effectiveness it must have? From what elements can we better understand the internal dynamics of a culture, its sagacity?

We certainly live in cultural contexts of hybridity, *mpuku-mu-nuni* (as a bat half rodent half bird) and *mamiwata*; one is neither completely in a context of orality nor exclusively in one of writing; neither in a context of secure cultural rootedness nor in that of a true understanding of the cultures of others (the wings). *Nlele wansompa ka utominanga makinu ko, mais, buabu makinu mayikidi kaka mansompa ye ma milele mia nsompa!* Even education no longer seems to start from the student's ecological environment or from his cultural environment. Do we ever ask: what are the most important virtues of one's culture?

The inhabitants of this country have experienced traumas of all kinds (the slave trade as victims and perpetrators, the forgotten Leopoldian holocaust, colonialism, racism and the Ota Benga case, senseless wars, the debt contracted without people's knowledge and impossible to repay leading to a new form of slavery, hostage taking by internal and external mafias, massacres, external impositions, parental repression, the thingification of women reduced to an office, etc.), their cultures would also have been shaped in the mastery of management or in the impossibility of managing (replaying) the effects of these traumas. The positive prohibitions internal to each culture seem to have given way, without rethinking the relationships of

---

[15] The *Mbongi a Nsi* was a political invention which Wamba-dia-Wamba inaugurated. It consisted of a number of meetings where a small number of militants discussed political questions of any kind after a guiding introduction. It was an attempt to adapt the rural Mbongi discussed below to an urban setting in order to develop a new form of political subjectivity that was based among the masses.

constancy: the essentiality of the mother-child relationship; the essentiality of the community (*kanda*, *Gemeinwesen*) and the fundamental character of the relationship with the rest of nature. All these essentialities seem to be in crisis. Parental repression, individualism (and witchcraft) and the withdrawal of totemism disturb all these essentialities. Hasn't harmful witchcraft taken precedence over that of protecting/defending the community? The initiations designed to reproduce the living-better-together-in-the-community seem to have disappeared. The *mvila*, the links of community solidarity *ne-Kongo* are no longer active. The prominence of the *biyinga* (the uninitiated) and the individualistic *babulua-meso* (*ndoki*) attest to the crisis of the community. Has not almost any living animal become a source of meat? The surviving fragments of cultures without any roots in the essentialities of constancy are only for decoration.

Cultural traditions are prescriptions for possible exit from within situations. When people are no longer interpellated by such prescriptions, choice within situations disappears and the horizon of freedom becomes narrowed if not fully closed. The prescriptions to exit from difficult situations become difficult to find. The dynamics of the palaver, for example, make it possible to revitalize this horizon by reactivating prescriptions and to broaden the field of freedom and therefore creativity. It is here, for example, that the *ngana zata bambuta* (the lessons learned by our ancestors, our ancient sages) become active prescriptions. Culturally uprooted people were referred to as *ka basala Bantu ko*; but, when the majority consists of the 'culturally uprooted', there is a crisis of the community and the emergence of a new community. Would not the retreat of the dynamics of the *Mbongi*, and especially that of the palaver, without any visible replacement, be one of the reasons for the difficulty we have in controlling our conflict situations? Are *nganda*, bars, television or churches a valid replacement? Don't street children attest, among other things, to the absence of the Mbongi's dynamics?

The root causes of the situation of hybridity

The fundamental Congolese (and African) problem is the relationship between the city and the countryside (the rural world); more particularly the failure to have developed the countryside where the majority of the population lives, the failure to have granted the rural population and the culture of rural areas the same capacities or powers as the people of the cities so that together they could reshape the whole society.

The lack of development of rural areas and the rural population is a heavy burden that tends to push the entire economy towards collapse. This is not just a question of economics; it is first and foremost a political question, one of the essential relations of the state, of political philosophy and of the direction taken by the whole civilization. This is not just a question of development policy; it concerns the need for new relations between urban and rural social classes; it is a new partnership in the management of state power between the people of the cities and those of the countryside. Neither the ruralization of cities nor the urbanization of the countryside will solve the problem. It is not a question of economic policy between the city and the countryside or between the government and the countryside, nor primarily a question of money, technology, investment or markets, but rather of specific types of relations between urban and rural social classes, specific political relations in the management of state power.

It is the orientation and prescriptions on the state which influence the functioning of the latter towards the vast majority of society, the peasantry, and towards the community ownership of land.

It is the nature of the African state itself that is the problem. It is a *state grafted* on the colonial one, a state that has not developed organically with the African social body, rooted in, and imbued with, African traditions and cultures. It is a Western and urban graft and exists in a largely non-industrialized, non-urban, poor, illiterate and rural society. Even political parties are grafts of the colonialist masters' institutions which have not emerged organically from the social body of African society. As in medicine, the social body tends to reject these transplants. The crude characteristics of African political life can be explained on this basis. This is also the root of the crisis of the African state. We must also add to this the impact on the psychology (individual and social) and on the mentality of Africans of the slave trade, colonialism and racism.

There is an urgent need to restructure the state so that it is in a healthy and organic relationship with the vast majority of the rural population which still lives within rural cultures. It is necessary to make it accountable to all this population for it to have a proportional impact on the state so that it may participate, on an equal footing with the urban population, in all the bodies and commissions through which decisions are taken regarding the whole of society. The state must be restructured so that it has a healthy relationship with the traditions, cultures and languages of the African peoples. We need an elite for the community of the countryside, as well as for the urban community, and not a self-appointed communitarian elite representing the countryside for the interests of its individual members.

This grafting has a long history from the violent rupture, in the West, of the real (natural, peasant) community in favor of an artificial community of capital. It was a break between a communal rationality and a rationality of capitalist calculation. Instead of seeking a synthesis and continuity between the past, the present and the future, there developed a tabula rasa. The discontinuity between the past and the present has created a psychological situation characteristic of an urban mentality that consciously or unconsciously sought to annihilate the past associated with rural culture and the rural population. The vicious and violent destruction of peasants and their culture in the formation of modern Western society, the absence of a continuity of peasant culture in modern Western culture and the failure to develop a synthesis between peasant culture and tradition on the one hand and modern urban culture, on the other hand, are at the root of what is experienced as an absence of meaning and depth in modern Western culture and its attendant personality. Hence the ontological primacy of the individual over society, which reduces the latter to a meeting or contract between isolated individuals.

The profound meaning of dictatorship in Africa is the imposition of this graft on the whole of society, by means that aim at the violent and vicious destruction of peasant culture and traditions. In the domain of medicine, such an imposition ultimately kills the body. This is not far from the violent destruction of native Americans to establish modern society in the US. It is a deep civilizational crisis. The three African refusals can be explained on this basis: the refusal to think for oneself, the refusal to take seriously all of one's past and the refusal to see things in a long-term perspective. We speak with borrowed speeches, sometimes without being aware of it.

We must get out of this problem where our so-called intellectuals are thoughtlessly and relentlessly dismissing African culture and thoughtlessly promoting Western culture. This path leads us to the cultural confusion that characterizes Africa's urban youth and the aspiring middle class. Debates on democracy that do not take this situation into account are only aimed at getting the transplant accepted, making it more acceptable to the people. In order to have an impact, these debates must be inscribed in the necessity for new political relations between the city and the countryside. It is necessary to re-activate the continuity and synthesis between the cultural past, the present and the future and it is necessary to aim at the restructuring of the current state so that it ceases to be a mere transplant.

Only on this basis will we be able to achieve 1) the industrialization of our country, 2) the African agrarian revolution, 3) development of Africa with the elimination of rural underdevelopment, 4) the reform and transformation of education so that African traditions, cultures and languages become the centre of the enterprise, the generalization of literacy and the availability of reading materials for the masses of the African population, 5) the development of the capacity of African elites to produce Africa-centric solutions to the weaning crises and the collapse of the economy as well as the serious crisis of massive unemployment. It must be emphasised that there is a global social crisis in Africa as well as in the West, a serious crisis of governance and accountability of the African state as well as of the Western state. This issue must be the subject of further discussions.

In order to discuss and expand this question of cultural continuity as the foundation of a hope for a way out of the Congolese global crisis, I propose a debate on the Mbongi considered as the central element of traditional cultural creativity.

The Mbongi and the palaver: places of cultural healing

The Mbongi is first and foremost the site of the cultural processes of a (village, lineage, clan, etc.) community. Broadly speaking, cultural reproduction, was secured through this place. It was a multifunctional site with a conception of multiplicity. Everything was held in common, while recognizing the fact that everyone spoke on their own behalf. The village without a Mbongi is a dead village; the one who does not participate in the Mbongi does not understand the dynamics of village life. The difficult intellectual work of mastering community struggles is undertaken at this site. For example, the importance of the Mbongi was emphasized by villagers, to the detriment of the missionaries who had not understood its symbolism of fire. As potential Christians, asked to choose between heaven and hell, villagers had all preferred hell!

The Mbongi presupposes the idea of a real community, of which it serves as a leading and deliberating organ. In Kongo culture, the basic cell can be considered the kanda. Many proverbs, prescriptions therefore, point to the centrality of this community. Here is a sample of relevant proverbs:

> *kanda mukutu*, the ontological primacy of the community over the individual;
>
> *kanda mutu*, the community is the head;
>
> *kanda wakandula biela bia kanda*, community stimulates people in the community;
>
> *kanda wakanda mambu*, the community foresees the possibility of problems and conflicts;
>
> *untela nkingu miankulu mia kanda kidi yazaya miampa*, tell me the old principles of the community to understand the new;
>
> *mbongo a kanda ka mbongo aku ko*, the community thing is not private (respect for the public entity);
>
> *mu kanda babo longa ye longwa*, education in the community is reciprocal;
>
> *nkingu mia kanda nkingu mia nsi*, the prescriptions of the community are the prescriptions of the country (the country is the people who live there);
>
> *kanda n'landa: bankaka kwenda bankaka kwiza*, the community dialectic—*dingo-dingo*— the community is in a process of constant renewal;
>
> *simbi bia kanda (bia nsi) mu kilombo binikukinanga*, the community leader is a fish in the water;
>
> *nga nzenza muntu katunga fu bia bwala*, the stranger cannot do the customs of the community;
>
> *kanda kandu, ka kiloswa, ka kisabwa*, the community is a taboo, it can neither be thrown away or worshipped;

kanda i (mbundani a) bafwa ye bamoyo, the community is the union of dead ancestors and living people; etc.

It is clear that the essential nature of the community is affirmed. The prescriptions concern the protection/reproduction of the community while the anti-values (*kindoki kia ndila*, destructive individualistic witchcraft) aim at its destruction. The settlement of community (social) relations is done by the Mbongi (the house without walls or the place of community transparency). There are also prescriptions, in the form of proverbs, that show the centrality of the Mbongi. Here is a sample from Kongo:

vata dikondolo mbongi vata diafwa, the community without a Mbongi is lifeless;

boko (Mbongi) wabokula mambu, the Mbongi rules the affairs of the community;

boko waboka mu vata, the Mbongi summons the village community meetings;

m*bila boko ni beto kulu*, the call of the Mbongi is addressed to all;

mbongi wabokila mambu, the Mbongi is a community commission of inquiry to regulate social relations;

lusanga (Mbongi) wasangumuna mambu, the Mbongi reveals/ exposes all the problems of the community in order to solve them;

lusanga (Mbongi) didi dia kimvuka, the mbongi is the leading nucleus of the community;

yemba (Mbongi) wayembamana mambu ma kanda, the Mbongi protects the affairs of the community;

nsamu katoma ku kioto (Mbongi) kabiya ku kioto, good or bad solutions, these end at the Mbongi;

kioto (Mbongi) kioko kia kanda kalambanga, the healing food of the community is prepared at the Mbongi; etc.

The *fu kia nsi* (constitution of the country) among the BaKongo first posited that there is first the community; there is no isolated individual; each person is always in front of a brother or sister in the presence of any person of the community; the multiple links woven between the members (of *mvila, ndonga, bivumu, totems, misibu, initiations*, etc.) attest to this. It is these privileged places between the members of kanda or between the *makanda* that must be protected at all costs against any conflict in order to ensure the continuity of fraternal, peaceful, and harmonious relations. The Mbongi is a daily practice for settling community relations.

The Mbongi is openness: anyone can come to the Mbongi to share what they can share with others: thought, wood, food, peanuts, cassava, drinks, etc. Even women come there occasionally; foreigners are welcome. The Mbongi therefore has as its horizon the pure and inconsistent multiplicity: the arrival of the stranger is expected. The rich, the poor, the eldest, the youngest, the *mfumu-dikanda* (the free person), the *muan'ambuta*, the *nsumbidi-nsumbidi* (the community slave), the *kisana* (the orphan), all are welcome at the Mbongi. Everyone speaks at the Mbongi in his (or her) own name which is both fundamentally communal and singular.

The Mbongi is singularization: even as a set of community ties, each person is distinguished, not only by his own definitional name or *ndusi* but according to the requirements of the situation that requires him to speak on his own behalf. The Mbongi counts everyone as they are and where they are.

The Mbongi is the sharing of tasks (roles) and their coordination. There is a leader of the Mbongi whose legitimacy depends on singularity, as the embodiment of community ties (tradition) and on the proper functioning of the settlement of community relations that protect the harmony of the community as preventative of conflicts.

All this is guided by the culture/subjectivity of ...*sana*: as in *zolasana, salasana, simbasana, natasana zitu, tungasana, longasana, vungasana, kabasana*, etc., attested by the fact that the ancestors watch over it.

Sometimes very serious conflicts could arise: those for which it was said that *nsinga dikanda ninga kaka uninganga kansi ka tabuka ko* (the community bond can vibrate with tension but it must not be broken) and those that can lead to the rupture of the community. Conflicts include those due to non-antagonistic contradictions among the people of the community as well as communitarian or inter-communitarian antagonistic contradictions. The conditions of existence of these conflicts are specified: the destructive action of witchcraft (*kindoki kia ndila*), the irresponsibility of the elite of the community (the *Nzonzi* for example) which may become a simple community elite, the external conditions favored by internal ones (the sorcerer from the without eats/kills in the community through the sorcerer within), *kimongi kia mayala* (forgetting public morality the *sana* and individualism), *kimuyeke*, etc.

The common way of resolving conflicts is through the palaver (communitarian or inter-communitarian *ntungasani*) where the whole community is challenged. The palaver is the generalized self-questioning of the whole community. The palaver is multi-functional: it addresses the detection of short circuits in community ties, the re-adjustment of the settlement of community relations, community healing, the judgment of the specific conflict that divides the community into opposing camps and the reconciliation of those camps (*ta bindokila*), the purification of community speech (destruction of bad words), the generalized community massage (mental, spiritual and psychological) in order to restore community health, and the lifting of prohibitions and their re-institution , etc.

The palaver is a very complex process. To guide such a process, there are *Nzonzi*, specialists or elites from the community, sages, dialecticians (witnesses of the compossibility of community truths and detectors of bad speech, bad looks, etc.), lawyers, healers, community massagers, 'coolers' of the community bond in tension, rhetoricians or masters of public speaking, etc. They don't just 'say the *fu kia nsi*' (i.e. say the law) which could be questioned. The *Nzonzi* must possess the art of public speaking nourished by community wisdom made of significant songs, ancestral dances, proverbs as secular wisdom concentrated in short locutions, the history and geography of the community environment, cultural elements not to be ignored, such as *mvila, bivumu, ndandani*, etc., and not only the ability to know how to speak the *fu kia ns*i (*kisinsi, kisivata, kisizunga, kisikanda*).

The palaver is not only the place of political processes that deal with matters of politics, that is to say the settlement of community relations, but it is also a place of participatory thought, in so far as thought is a relation to the real that the palaver requires. It can be said that the *Nzonzi* are militants of these processes. A few rules guide these processes: these include exposing secrets (yalula nsala) and especially the ones that are the most dangerous such as evil witchcraft, maintaining transparency (*wata ngana bangula ngana, kibongi kia ngana walembana zo bangula, wafwila mu zingana*, the proverb is said to clarify the thought of things, he who said proverbs to confuse people, died of the confusion thus created), fully freeing speech (everyone capable of speaking has the right to speak), a repeated multiple dialogue (*multilogue*) (*mbo nge ni yandi kwandi batalanga?* Why is it only him that we must see, hear, listen to..?), maintaining the ethics of truth (*nzonzi za luvunu, ngo..!*), taking the point of view of the *res publica* (*mu kanda kingenga kia mambu kuanana* and then, *nto wayenda buka-ka wakondama*) (not only do we respond to the speech with a speech (B. Pascal), we need an adversarial debate - *bana batedi, bana baseku-di*), recognizing that truths are multiple (*mfumu na mfumu, nganga na nganga* - the political is measured with the political, the scholar is measured with the scholar), preparing his interventions using, when necessary, the meetings in commissions (*mfundu*), resorting to everything that can explain, inspire, persuade (the *ndozi ndotolongo*, the thesis song, the poem, the theater and the bodily gestures), Finally, this amounts to practicing the idea that people think.

I have studied elsewhere the concrete course of a palaver.[16] It must be said that the nature of the conflict that requires a palaver determines the concrete form it takes. It can be a kind of court process between two parties, individuals, families or groups of people. The whole community, with its notables, is constituted in a court (*mbasi-a-nkanu*). The mfundu take the form of commissions (*mfundu za luzengo and mfundu za bindokila*). Each party gives itself one or more *Nzonzis* serving as its official spokesmen. Sometimes the palaver takes place at the chief of the village's place who is generally respected and respectable and who is a moral authority accepted by all.

Very briefly, what are the most important cultural values that emerge from the study of the Mbongi and the palaver? First, there is the sacredness of the ancestral land, without which the community loses its integrity. The central vision that motivates the whole community is to let life live (*dingo-dingo*, life is a process of uninterrupted

---

[16] See Wamba-dia-Wamba 'Experiences of Democracy in Africa: Reflections on Practices of Communalist Palaver as a Social Method of Resolving Contradictions among the People, Philosophy and Social Action XI (3) 1985. See also https://www.newframe.com/archive-communalist-palaver/ accessed 01/11/2021

change), to live and make live the community to live better: everything for the community and nothing against the community, but second also the sovereignty of all human life. The fundamental crimes are the alienation of ancestral land (*wateka ntoto dikanda neti ngororo/vangu* - he who sells ancestral land carries his mortal cross). The *mukongo* (the Kongo person) carries a crime (*nata nkanu*, a behaviour) but does not commit a crime. The crime has its roots in the functioning of the community; the former cannot be corrected without also correcting the latter. Individual wealth is suspected to be an unjust enrichment (*kimvwama kia muyeke*). Such a rich man must either be killed or exposed to bad luck (*lokwa*). It is the *kimvwama kia kanda* (*difwa dia kanda, mvwilu ya kanda*, necessary for *landa nsamu mia kanda*) that was preferred. The community does not put its trust in the rich man since he tends to be partisan (*mvwama nsusu, kanuana, maki mandi katanini*, the rich one among the hens, if she fights, it is to defend her eggs.)

Failure to properly/fairly represent the community beyond its boundaries (*kintumwa kia maghubi/ kinimalonde* or diplomacy) was viewed as high treason punishable by public death in the market. Politics being of the collective (*kinzonzi kia kanda; kia kingenga, bakulu ka basisa kio ko*, but also: *munwa umosi kitutu,* a single mouth is an empty calabash), a diplomatic mission was a dangerous function to perform. This is perhaps why it is said that politics is undertaken in the name of the ancestors (*ngana zata bambuta vo*). Finally, the question is: who do you serve when all is said and done?

The ideology of *sana*, namely living for others, community solidarity was, as is also accepted today, the foundation of peace. It is also this ideology that demands that conflicts can only be resolved through the palaver, with the active participation of the whole community (*wadia wadia, tala nkubu yaku, nkubu yaku, lumbu kikabaka, ngangu, ngangu ziyokele!*)

The teachings of the mbongi (and palaver) today

The Mbongi is increasingly disappearing in the villages without there being anything to replace it. Along with it, language in the Kongo countryside is threatened with extinction, particularly here in Kinshasa. The main sources of influence (in crisis) in the formation of youth today (the family, the school, the Church, television, the street) do not include the Mbongi. Initiation practices (*ku kanga, ku kongo, ku londe*) seem to have disappeared. Individualism reigns supreme in its cultural ignorance.

Our Transitional Constitution opens with a reference, in its preamble, to the 'cultural and spiritual values deeply rooted in the traditions of solidarity and justice of the Congolese people' and to the awareness 'of cultural diversity which is a factor of spiritual enrichment of the personality of our People'. This consciousness does not seem to be expressed in the rest of the Constitution. The Congolese cultural anchoring of so-called universal values is not specified. It would be interesting for example to make a *ne-Kongo* cultural reading of this Constitution.

The primacy of the community over the individual does not seem to be affirmed. It would be important to explain the cultural foundation of these transitional institutions: a total Western rooting or a total African rooting? Professor B. Mupinganayi (Intercongolese Dialogue, 2002) speaks of 'political unculture', what if it was 'cultural unculture' only? There is nothing in the transitional institutions to prevent individuals from pursuing their personal interests as a matter of priority.

Cotinho's attempt to create a Mbongi on the theme of 'save the Congo' was violently suppressed. His call to all to participate in a palaver at the May 20 stadium had worried the government terribly. Pastor Cotinho, persecuted by pastors close to the state, was beaten; his life was only saved by the grace of God.

The whole political vision, rooted in the grafted state, is focused solely on the (especially individual) conquest of power subordinating into the background the promotion and protection of all human life. While the majority of the population demands that institutions work in favour of society as a whole, they only work in favour of certain individuals. The search for 'commissions', in the very execution of the obligations assigned to animators, blocks the realization of projects (for example: the resolution of the electricity crisis in Kinshasa and the evacuation of garbage) favorable to the whole community. Serving the people has become a favour rather than an obligation.

People talk a lot about democracy as a 'universal politics' (by which they mean Western politics). This is because they do not take into account the cultural or historical foundation of actually existing democracies. American democracy was built on the basis of eliminating/ excluding native Americans, relegating Blacks to the margins, celebrating the gains of the European bourgeois revolutions, and on dominating the rest of the world. The British, the oldest democracy, remains marked by its history and its cultural foundation, up to the self-confidence characterized by the absence of a written constitution. No form of democracy is uniquely universal.

When the dialectic of the wings becomes detached from that of the roots, Afonso 1ˢᵗ rather than Mpanzu succeeds King Nzinga Nkuwu, and Nzadi becomes Zaire without us noticing the mystification, Kongo central becomes Bas-Congo. (*Ukwela mama, tata kwandi, kanele vo lauki?*)

For the lack of real *zimbongi*, congolese society as such, or even its parts, have not taken in hand the settlement of its social relations disturbed by conflicts. People talk of the absence of a state in some parts of the country (in Ituri, for example), the fact is rather that it is cultural sites for the settlement of social or community relations that are lacking. The grafted state, without any cultural roots, can only impose itself by force. Are there no cultural foundations of the actions of those who facilitate the plundering of our national resources by foreigners?

What are the cultural foundations that guided the inter-Congolese negotiations as to the choice of participants, mediators, facilitators or of the venue? When we fall into a hole, we do not look at the cultural colour of the one who comes to our aid, perhaps... But once out of the hole?

Tomorrow the Mbongi:
Furthering of subjection or independence?

The question of the Mbongi is the question of the effective participation of the entire Congolese people in the settlement of the social relations of the whole of Congolese society. The gradual disappearance of the Mbongi in the village means that the idea of 'every man for himself' has taken over the city. The moral values of respect, of the ideology of *sana*, of the sacredness of the ancestral earth, etc., have fallen away if not completely disappeared. Children no longer learn anything regarding cultural values, for example, the democratic experience of participating in the *ntungasani* debate on one's own behalf and of demanding the reaffirmation of one's rights. Institutions, which are essentially bureaucratic - including schools in the hands of self-confident teachers - provide no education for democracy. If the grafted state manages to uproot all traditional cultural values in order to replace them, the country will remain under guardianship.

Independence requires the existence of *zimbongi* through whom people can think together and can regulate social relations. The transformation of repressive social relations into non-repressive relations depends on this and not solely on the conquest of the grafted state power even by the best among us.

Time will tell.

Notes

www.ingramcontent.com/pod-product-compliance
Lightning Source LLC
Chambersburg PA
CBHW060522280326
41933CB00014B/3070

* 9 7 8 1 9 9 0 2 6 3 3 3 0 *